101 Creepy Creature Jokes

by Jovial Bob Stine
Illustrated by B.K. Taylor

SCHOLASTIC INC.
New York Toronto London Auckland Sydney

ISBN 0-590-43171-4

Copyright © 1990 by Robert L. Stine.
Illustrations copyright © 1990 by Scholastic Inc.
All rights reserved. Published by Scholastic Inc.

12 11   6 7 8/9

Printed in the U.S.A.   01

First Scholastic printing, October 1990

MONSTER MADNESS

First Monster: Why did you eat those tightrope walkers?
Second Monster: I like a well-balanced diet!

Why do ghosts shiver and moan?

It's drafty under that sheet!

Girl Monster: Mom, the teacher said
I was nice, smart, and well-behaved.
Mother Monster: Don't feel bad,
dear. You'll do better next semester.

Boy Monster: Look how much I've eaten — practically the whole family. Ma, I've eaten the mother, the brother, the sister, and the grandparents. Now, I'm going after the pop!

Mother Monster: Put him down, son. You know pop is bad for your teeth.

What did the monster kid say when he saw Santa Claus?

"Yum, yum!"

Why do werewolves howl up at the full moon?

Because you can't howl down at the full moon!

Why did the zombie stay home from the party?

He was dead tired.

Why do vampires drink blood?

Root beer makes them burp!

What's the zombie's favorite subject?

Latin, because it's a dead language.

What do you call a disgusting, slime-dripping, two-headed monster who comes to New York for the first time?

A tourist.

What did the vampire from outer space say when he landed on Earth?

"Take me to your bleeder!"

What is ten feet tall, has two heads, and goes click-click?

A ballpoint monster!

What do you get if you cross King Kong with a kangaroo?

Big holes in the ground!

MONSTER MOMMIES

Girl Monster: Mommy, the kids all say I'm a werewolf. That's not true, is it?

Mother Monster: Of course not. Now shut up and comb your face!

Girl Monster: Mommy, I hate my friend's guts.

Mother Monster: Then leave them on the side of the plate and eat the rest of your dinner.

Boy Monster: Mommy, the kids at school all laugh at me and say I'm a monster and my head is too big. That's not true, is it?

Mother Monster: Of course not. Go get me some things at the supermarket. I want fifteen pounds of onions, twelve pounds of potatoes, five cabbages, and two watermelons.

Boy Monster: Okay, Mommy. Where's the shopping cart?

Mother Monster: It's broken. Just put everything in your cap.

Daughter Monster: Mommy, my friend Susie says I'm a vampire. That's not true, is it?

Mother Monster: Of course not. Vampires suck blood. You didn't suck her blood, did you?

Daughter Monster: Well . . . only once or twice.

Son: Mommy, the kids at school all say I eat like a monster. That's not true, is it?

Mother: Of course not. But how many times do I have to tell you to stop eating with your hands and use a shovel?

Girl Monster: Mommy, the kids all say we're aliens from outer space. That's not true, is it?

Mother Monster: Vegl dibrogmrn di shturtl mixtor!

Boy Monster: Mommy, the kids all say I'm a two-headed monster. That's not true, is it?

Mother Monster: Shut your mouths. I'm trying to work.

BOYS AND GHOULS

Why does the boy monster kiss the girl monster on the back of her neck?

He has to. That's where her lips are!

Boy Monster: You have such lovely blue eyes.
Girl Monster: What's the matter? Don't you like my green eyes and my red eyes?

Boy Werewolf: I just love your hair. Is that a new hairdo?
Girl Werewolf: No, I just forgot to comb my face this morning!

Boy Monster: Did you get the big, red heart I sent you for Valentine's Day?
Girl Monster: Yes, I did. Thank you.
Boy Monster: Is it still beating?

Boy Vampire: I just love your type.
Girl Vampire: Really? What type am I?
Boy Vampire: RH-positive.

How does one monster greet another monster that has yellow skin with big, red sores all over it, has six green eyes with pus dripping from them, and is drooling purple slime from its three mouths?

"Hey, good-looking!"

Why are boy and girl skeletons
cowards?

They don't have any guts!

First Vampire: Why did you fall in love with Count Dracula?

Second Vampire: I guess it was love at first bite!

First Vampire: Where are you going to take Nancy on your date?

Second Vampire: Oh, I thought we'd go to the movies, and then out for a quick bite!

SOME FRANKENSTEIN FUN

What did Frankenstein think of his own creation?

He thought it was shocking!

What does Frankenstein have for lunch?

About two thousand volts.

What do you call a monster who flies a kite in a lightning storm?

Benjamin Franklinstein.

Bride of Frankenstein: I bought
   you a new chair for your birthday.
Frankenstein: Oh, thanks. I can't
   wait to plug it in!

Was the Frankenstein monster a hit?

Yes. He was a staggering success!

What's Frankenstein's favorite TV show?

A Current Affair.

What's a good way to greet Frankenstein?

"Hi, there. Watts new?"

What's green, weighs four hundred pounds, and has eight wheels?

Frankenstein on roller skates.

Why was Frankenstein arrested for throwing a party?

He threw it across the Grand Canyon!

Why did Frankenstein eat a box of bullets?

He wanted to grow bangs!

Why did Frankenstein go to a psychiatrist?

He had a screw loose.

What is green, has bolts on the sides of his neck, and is two feet tall?

Frankenstein bending over to tie his shoelaces.

CREATURE FEATURES

What do you call a dizzy demon?

A wobblin' goblin.

What do you call a monster's oatmeal?

Ghoul gruel.

What do you call a very clean ghost?

A neat sheet.

What do you call a vampire that King Kong sits on?

A flat bat.

What do you call a skeleton who's always bragging?

A bony phony.

What do you call a monster in the classroom?

A creature teacher.

What do you call a person who makes movies about ghosts?

A specter director.

What do you call a fairy tale that a monster tells his child?

A gory story.

What do you call a monster who's always hatching plots?

A schemin' demon.

What do you call a friendly Egyptian tomb-dweller?

A chummy mummy.

What do you call a mummy who eats crackers in bed?

A crummy mummy.

What do you call a monster that King Kong folds in half?

A creased beast.

What do you call a person who loves to go into haunted houses?

A shriek freak.

What do you call a monster who is
ten feet tall?

Shorty!

HOWLS & HOWLERS

What's convenient and weighs twenty thousand pounds?

A monster snack-pack.

Reporter: Why did you take this movie part, Count Dracula?
Dracula: It's a role I can really sink my teeth into!

Mr. Monster: I'm starved.
Mrs. Monster: I just put dinner into the microwave.
Mr. Monster: Oh good. Who is it?

What is the ghost's favorite car?

Boo-icks!

Why does Godzilla have such a long neck?

Because his head is so far from his body!

What do you call a monster who was locked in a freezer overnight?

A cool ghoul!

Reporter: Did you enjoy the movie, Mr. Frankenstein?

Frankenstein: Yes, it kept me in stitches!

Mother Monster: You've been fighting again. You've lost all your teeth.

Boy Monster: No, I haven't, Mom. I have them right here in my pocket.

Why did the mama monster scold her
son for eating people?

*He was supposed to save his dessert
for last!*

Why did the werewolf attack the
streetlight?

He wanted a light bite!

What did the monster say when he
slammed the door on his hand?

"Ouch!"

What kind of necklace did the mummy give his girlfriend?

A choker.

First Monster: See that monster over there? He's not very good at math.
Second Monster: Why do you say that?
First Monster: He can't count to forty without taking his shoes off.

First Monster: You don't have a brain in your head.
Second Monster: Which head?

Boy Monster: You have the most beautiful blue eyes I've ever seen.
Girl Monster: You really like them? Here. You wear them for a while so I can see how they look!

What does a ghost eat for breakfast?

Scream of Wheat!

Clerk: Would you like to make a
  donation to the blood bank, sir?
Vampire: No. Just browsing.

Monster: Hey, waiter — there's only one fly in my soup!

45

DON'T CROSS THESE MONSTERS!

What would you get if you crossed a werewolf with a dozen eggs?

A very hairy omelette.

What would you get if you crossed a vampire with a gazelle?

A quick bite.

What would you get if you crossed
Frankenstein with a thirty-foot-long
electric eel?

A shock.

What do you get if you cross a
monster?

Big trouble!

What would you get if you crossed a
ghost with a dessert chef?

Boo-berry pie.

What would you get if you crossed a vampire with a vampire?

A vampire. (What else??)

What would you get if you crossed a monster with a monster?

A monster. (You were expecting Pee-wee Herman??)

What would you get if you crossed a mummy with a CD?

A wrap song.

What would you get if you crossed a garbage heap with The Blob?

A bigger garbage heap.

What would you get if you crossed a skeleton with a watermelon?

A watermelon for which you have to spit out the bones.

What would you get if you crossed a werewolf with a washing machine?

A wash-and-werewolf.

What would you get if you crossed Godzilla with a hitchhiker?

A two-and-a-half-ton pickup.

An alien sat down in a restaurant and quickly ate the plate and the silverware. "That's what I like about these fast-food restaurants," he said. "They have the food right at your table when you sit down!"

MORE FAVORITES

What is the ghost's favorite TV game show?

Squeal of Fortune.

What's the werewolf's favorite fairy tale?

Little Red Riding Hood — except for the unhappy ending.

What is the ghost's favorite book series?

Sheet Valley High.

What is the werewolf's favorite hotel?

Howliday Inn.

What is the vampire's favorite city?

Great Neck, Long Island.

What is the vampire's favorite part of a horse race?

When the horses are neck and neck!

Who is the monster's favorite comedian?

Blob Newhart.

Who is the monster's favorite comedienne?

Hairy Tyler Moore.

When Godzilla goes out for dinner, what's his favorite food?

The restaurant.

What's Frankenstein's favorite
baseball event?

The All-Scar Game.

What's the ghost's favorite magazine?

Good Housecreeping.

What's the witch's favorite subject in school?

Spelling.

Who is the ghost's favorite movie
star?

Boo Derek.

Who is the zombie's favorite movie
star?

Robert Deadford.

Who is the zombie's favorite
funnyman?

Deddy Murphy.

MONSTERS IN SCHOOL

Why did the monster flunk math?

He subtracted the teacher.

Why did Dr. Jekyll flunk chemistry?

He kept drinking the final exam.

Where can you find ghosts in your school?

On the scarecases!

What kind of grades did the headless horseman get?

Incomplete!

What kind of school did King Kong go to?

A high school — a very high school!

Why did the monster like geography better than math?

The geography book had more pages and took longer to eat.

What instrument did the skeleton play in the school band?

Trom-bone.

Why did the ghost become a cheerleader?

She liked to show off her school spirit.

What was the monster's favorite school subject?

Home ecccccch.

What did the abominable snowman
think of the movie?

It left him cold.

First Invisible Man: Nice not to see
you again.
Second Invisible Man: Nice not to
see you again, too!

GIGGLES AND GASPS!

Young Monster: Mmmmphh ggmmmmmppph mmmmppppph.
Mama Monster: Junior, how many times do I have to tell you not to talk with someone in your mouth!

Vampire (on phone): Hello, city morgue?
Clerk: Yes, it is.
Vampire: Do you deliver?

What's soft and cuddly and bites your neck?

A teddy bat.

Three zombies were about to play cards in a graveyard. "Hey," said one of them. "Murray isn't here. We can't play cards with just three of us."

"Okay," said one of his zombie friends. "Let's dig up another player."

First Zombie: I'd like to take you out.

Second Zombie: Over my dead body!

Pet-Store Clerk: Shall I put your new kittens in a carrying case for you, sir?

Monster: No, thanks. I'll eat them here.

One Vampire to Another: You look familiar. Haven't I bitten you somewhere before?

Famous Artist: Today I am going to begin my sculpture of an alien from outer space.

Reporter: How interesting. How do you sculpt an alien from outer space?

Famous Artist: It's easy. You get a block of granite and cut away everything that doesn't look like an alien!

Newspaper Reporter (interviewing a monster): Does having two heads make life difficult for you?

Monster: Yes and no.

What does a werewolf do that people step into?

Pants.

What did the zombie child call his father?

Deady.

What time is it when Frankenstein
starts to shovel snow?

Wintertime.

A young monster nervously approached his girlfriend's father. "Sir," he said cautiously, "I've come to ask for your daughter's hand."

"Nonsense," said the monster father. "Either you take all of her, or just forget about it!"

What did the judge say when The
Blob came into the courtroom?

"Odor in the court!"

Wife: Louie, are you awake? There's
a monster downstairs in the living
room!
Husband: No, I'm asleep.

Who sleeps all day, bites necks, and puts out forest fires?

Smoky the Vampire.

Young Monster: Mother, may I leave the table?
Mother Monster: No. Finish it, dear. You need fiber.

What has two hundred legs, one hundred heads, and horns?

A *monster marching band.*

THESE RHYMES ARE A SCREAM!

There once was a werewolf named
   Dwight,
Whose computer was his constant
   delight.
But when the full moon was seen,
Dwight would eat his machine.
You see, his bark was much worse
   than his byte!

A very timid monster named Clark
Daily ate kids in the park.
But from evening to dawn,
Kids played on the lawn.
They knew Clark was afraid of the
   dark!

There once was a werewolf named
  June
Who refused to howl at the moon.
When attacked by a mob
For not doing her job,
She said, "Sorry, I can't carry a tune."

A peckish vampire named Breck
Could not keep his appetite in check.
Said he, "If I ever invite you,
I'm certain to bite you.
Let's face it, I'm a pain in the neck!"

There once was a monster named
    Brute,
Whose face, it was really a beaut.
But his girl, Miss Godzilla,
Made everyone ill-a.
Compared to her, Brute was cute!

Boxing Trainer: You're the greatest monster boxer who ever lived. Look at you — you're terrifying! You've got nine bulging eyes; four huge, runny noses; and five enormous, slobbering mouths. So why do you want to give up boxing?

Monster: I don't want to ruin my looks.

MORE CREATURE CROSSES!

What would you get if you crossed a zombie with the family car?

A dead battery.

What do you get when you cross a werewolf with a cow?

A hamburger that bites back.

What happens when you cross a vampire with a hotdog roll?

A fangfurter!

LAST SHRIEKS!

Reporter: Mr. Godzilla, you've practically eaten that entire hotel. But why did you leave the top five floors?

Godzilla: My doctor told me to cut down on suites!

Jack: Is it true that a vampire won't harm you if you carry a clove of garlic?

Jill: That depends on how many miles away from the vampire you are when you carry the garlic!

Why is The Blob considered a great
  artist?

He draws flies.

Reporter: Did you enjoy the rock band, Mr. Werewolf?

Werewolf: Yes. The drummer was a bit tough, but everyone else was delicious!

Reader: That last joke of yours was two thirds of a pun.

Jovial Bob: What do you mean?

Reader: P.U.